XOXO
A COCKTAIL BOOK

AN UNOFFICIAL
GOSSIP GIRL
FAN BOOK

Bridget
THORESON

 ULYSSES PRESS

Published in the U.S. by:
Ulysses Press
P.O. Box 3440
Berkeley, CA 94703
www.ulyssespress.com

ISBN: 978-1-64604-042-1
Library of Congress Control Number: 2020931879

Printed in China by Tian Hong Printing through Four Colour Print Group
10 9 8 7 6 5 4 3 2 1

Acquisitions editor: Casie Vogel
Managing editor: Claire Chun
Editor: Renee Rutledge
Proofreader: Kate St.Clair
Cover design: Malea Clark-Nicholson
Cover art: skyline © Malea Clark-Nicholson; background © Bokeh Blur
    Background/shutterstock.com
Interior design: Jake Flaherty
Interior photos: see page 190

Contents

Introduction

Hey Upper East Siders, Gossip Girl here...

Kristen Bell first uttered those words in 2007, and changed the world forever. I watched the first season in my college dorm room in the Bronx—just a couple miles but light-years away from the drama portrayed on-screen. I was older than the characters (but not the actors) on the show, and insanely unfamiliar with the glittering life they inhabited in the glittering city I shared. So, it became a guilty pleasure, a show I couldn't relate to but enjoyed watching for the allure, the travel, the 1% fantasy, and of course the mid-aughts fashion (do school uniforms even count if you can wear the tie open to your chest and swap in a sequin skirt?).

It had been years since I'd last watched *Gossip Girl* (since 2012 when I binged the entire first season again with my roommate in Brooklyn) when I heard there was a reboot in the works. The team at Ulysses Press immediately knew we needed to do something to pay homage to such an iconic show—because whether you love it or hate it or never even watched it, it is iconic. Everyone in America born after 1980 knows the significance of the words "you know you love me."

The project was clear right away: it had to be cocktails. *Gossip Girl* and cocktails—the two were inextricably linked. Booze was practically a main character on the show, rarely going two consecutive scenes without an appearance.

And so, in the chapters that follow, you'll find 100 of the world's most classic and delicious cocktails reimagined for *Gossip Girl* fans. There are fruity tropical drinks for the most decadent of spring breaks, moody bourbon cocktails for sipping in dark corners of indulgent clubs and classic martinis for nursing at home as you binge season after season, soaking up gin and glamour. This book celebrates all that *Gossip Girl* is through the lens of Manhattan's favorite accessory—a glass.

Chapters are arranged based on the main spirit used, except the last chapter, in which you'll find a small handful of delicious mocktails. Because let us never forget—while the legal drinking age has no bearing on the teenaged elite of Manhattan, for the rest of us, it does. We should always remember that until season five, most of the GG characters weren't actually legal, despite the hundreds of martinis, Scotch and sodas, and more martinis they're spotted drinking.

I know you'll love it.

XOXO

CHAPTER 1

A Bar Worthy of the Upper East Side

GLASSWARE

All gadgets and dodads aside, glassware is the real foundation of any bar. Glassware comes in tons of different shapes and sizes, some more versatile and some designed to serve a very specific purpose for just one or two kinds of drinks. While the glass doesn't necessarily make or break a good cocktail, it certainly adds to the experience and can take a great cocktail that extra notch higher. Not to mention, Manhattan's elite are all about the aesthetic, and serving a cocktail in the wrong glass is a fireable faux pas for any UES cater waiter.

I've outlined some of the basic and most versatile types of glasses here. At a minimum, I recommend keeping a set of wine glasses, rocks glasses, and cocktail or martini glasses, though you can build your collection as you expand and experiment with your bar.

MUST-HAVE GLASSWARE

Champagne flute or coupe—fairly self-explanatory for anyone familiar with Manhattan's elite, as there's no shortage of Champagne at even the simplest of events. Flutes are tall, narrow glasses with a curved bowl tapering up to a slightly narrower opening, designed to keep bubbles intact by reducing the surface area of the beverage. A coupe is a shorter, squatter stemmed glass, mostly used for visual purposes, since the wider rim is less effective at keeping bubbly bubbly. But, of course, the

Gatsby-esque aesthetic does have its advantages. Most cocktails that require bubbly will be served in a flute or coupe.

Cocktail glass—a stemmed glass with a V-shaped bowl and a wide opening. Use a cocktail glass for cocktails that are served "up"; that is, shaken or stirred, but served without ice.

Collins glass or highball—Collins glasses and highballs are often used interchangeably. Both are tall, cylindrical glasses used to serve drinks (such as a Tom Collins, a mojito, or a Bloody Mary) over ice, and often with a higher percentage of mixers. A Collins is slightly larger than a highball.

Irish coffee glass— a small footed glass mug with a handle used for Irish coffees, hot toddies, and other warm punches.

Martini glass—a martini glass is very similar to, and often used interchangeably with, a cocktail glass. However, a true, traditional martini glass will have a more acute V and a slightly flared, conical shape.

Rocks glass (old-fashioned)—very familiar to Upper East Siders, a rocks, or old-fashioned, glass is a short, squat glass. Frequently used to serve drinks over ice (or on the rocks), or drinks built in the glass rather than in a cocktail shaker, the glass is designed with a heavy bottom to stand up to muddling. Old-fashioneds, Mint Juleps, and Negronis are all served in a rocks glass, though Scotch, neat, makes the most common appearance in this glassware on the UES.

 Margarita glass—a shallow-bowled, wide-rimmed glass used mainly for margaritas and other frozen beverages. The shallowness of the glass doesn't lend itself to safely sipping a fully liquid drink, so reserve this for blended beverages.

 Shot glass—short, squat, and sturdy, a shot glass holds about 1.5 ounces—just enough to swallow in one gulp and slam on the bar. I haven't included many shot recipes (to be honest, if you're taking a shot, it's probably straight tequila), but this is useful in a home bar to serve as a measure, if you don't have a separate jigger.

 **Red wine glass**—a stemmed glass with a wider bowl and a narrower top, to allow the aromas of the wine to collect and funnel toward the drinker's nose. There are many different subtypes of wine glasses, but I recommend starting with a basic red and a basic white shape. If you want to keep only one set on hand, go for red over white—it's a more versatile shape. Though everyone on the UES seems to have the same set of square wine glasses, I don't recommend this. While it looks trendy, a real wine enthusiast knows that particular shape does nothing in service of the wine. Resist the urge to buy a funky shape—you'll regret it more than that backslide with your ex.

White wine glass—also tall and stemmed, but white wine glasses are narrower and have less of a size variation from bowl to lip. The smaller shape is meant to help preserve the chill on a white wine (for proper wine serving temperatures, see page 18).

TAKING CARE OF GLASSWARE

Even if you don't spend a fortune on your glassware, you'll want to take a couple of steps to keep it in good condition and effectively supporting your mixology. I don't recommend putting your glassware through the dishwasher, for risk of breaking. Hand wash the glasses carefully with warm water and mild soap, though I recommend using a detergent made specifically for glass. Don't use steel wool or an abrasive sponge, or risk scratches. Let the glasses air dry upside down or hand dry with a lint-free towel to avoid water spots. For the highest presentation, you can polish your glasses using steam or a clean coffee filter.

YOUR BAR'S FOUNDATION

Spotted: a bar cart worthy of the Upper East Side. A wide variety of cocktails often call for a wide variety of ingredients, from simple vodka to off-the-beaten-path crème de violette. But it must be your lucky day, because I've laid out everything you need, whether you're a beginner hosting your first sleepover or you're a seasoned entertainer throwing a lavish bash.

FOR A HIGH SCHOOL SLEEPOVER

❖ Flavored vodkas (orange, vanilla, coffee)

❖ Gin

❖ Rum (light, gold, spiced, coconut)

❖ Tequila

❖ Triple sec, Cointreau, orange liqueur

❖ Vodka

❖ Whiskey

FOR A BLACK TIE CHARITY GALA
(all of the above and):

❖ Amaretto

❖ Bourbon

❖ Brandy (regular, apple apricot)

❖ Cachaça

❖ Cognac

❖ Mezcal

❖ Rum (dark)

❖ Scotch and bourbon

FOR A SINFUL MASQUERADE PARTY
(all of the above and):

❖ Absinthe

❖ Bacardi 151

❖ Moonshine

❖ Rye

LIQUEURS AND OTHER

❖ Anise liqueur (like sambuca or similar)

❖ Beer

❖ Bitters (Angostura, Peychaud's, aromatic)

❖ Blue curaçao

❖ Campari or Aperol

XOXO A COCKTAIL BOOK

- Cherry whiskey
- Cinzano
- Cognac
- Crème de cacao
- Crème de cassis
- Crème de violette
- Drambuie
- Fernet-Branca, or other amaro
- Frangelico
- Galliano liqueur
- Ginger beer
- Irish cream
- Kahlua, or other coffee liqueur
- Maraschino liqueur
- Peach schnapps
- Peppermint schnapps
- Pimm's No. 1
- Prosecco, Champagne
- Raspberry liqueur (such as Chambord)
- Sake
- Sloe gin
- St-Germain liqueur
- Strawberry liqueur
- Vermouth (dry, extra dry, and sweet; Martini Rosso vermouth)
- White crème de menthe

GARNISHES

- Cinnamon sticks
- Citrus (limes, lemons, oranges)
- Eggs
- Fruit (peaches, raspberries, strawberries, blueberries)
- Green olives
- Honey
- Maraschino cherries
- Mint
- Sugar (cubes, sanding sugar)

MIXERS

- Agave nectar
- Blood orange juice
- Cola
- Cranberry juice
- Espresso
- Ginger ale
- Grapefruit juice
- Grenadine
- Orange juice
- Passion fruit juice or nectar
- Pineapple juice
- Rose's lime juice
- Seltzer, club soda, or tonic
- Simple syrup
- Sugar cane syrup

BASIC TOOLS

Any high society soiree needs three things: the perfect guest list, a star chef, and free-flowing booze. It may seem like your glass fills itself when you're a socialite, but behind every good cocktail is a great bartender and their arsenal of tools. With the basics I've laid out below, you'll be well on your way to hosting a cocktail hour worthy of even the poshest of charity galas.

Absinthe spoon—not too many cocktails call for absinthe, but if you feel like indulging in a dance with the green fairy, you'll need an absinthe spoon. They are typically shaped like a trowel and have holes in the middle. You'll rest the spoon over your glass of absinthe, place a sugar cube on top, and pour water over to let the sugar water drip slowly.

Bar spoon—a teaspoon with an extra-long handle. Basic, but crucial for mixing ingredients in tall glasses.

Blender—the odd colada never hurt anyone, and no one likes a frozen margarita with ice chunks.

Cocktail shaker—the best cocktail shakers will be metal (to quickly chill), have a tightly fitted top to prevent drips, and include a built-in strainer. Look for one that holds at least 16 ounces so your ingredients have room to mix and combine. You could opt for a "Boston shaker," which is a glass pint glass and a metal cup fitted tightly together.

Corkscrew—I know that when you opt for wine, nine times out of ten, it'll be champagne. But for those instances when you need a Chateau Petrus or have a guest who insists on Sancerre, keep at least one corkscrew handy. I recommend a basic double-hinged wine key over fancier (or, god forbid, battery-operated) versions.

Decanter—if your Sancerre-loving guest asks you to decant their white before serving, please send them away and never speak to them again. For bigger red wines, though, it is handy to have a decanter around. Pour the wine and let it sit to open up, soften the tannins, and aerate the wine (for more on this, see the Serving Wine section on page 16). You might also want a stoppered decanter to store Scotch if you feel upper crust, or just if it matches your bar cart vibe.

Jigger—the most crucial of bar tools. While you can use a standard shot glass in a pinch, a jigger is the best way to measure your cocktail ingredients. Usually shaped like an hourglass, this handy tool measures 1 ounce on one end and 1.5 ounces on the other. Most cocktails are about the proportions rather than the amount of an ingredient. A jigger will help you precisely portion out your elements.

Mixing glass—any tall glass that is big enough to stir (not shake) ingredients in. You can also use this tool as the bottom half of your Boston shaker.

Muddler—a wooden or plastic masher used to smash herbs, citrus, or other ingredients against the bottom of a glass (as in a Mint Julep). This helps release aromas or essential oils to allow for better flavor.

Paring knife and small cutting board—to cut citrus for twisting, juicing, or garnishing.

Strainer—if you go for a Boston shaker over a cocktail shaker, you'll definitely need a strainer, but it's good to have one on hand either way. A strainer will be crucial in making sure no extra ice gets into your drink to water it down.

STORING, OPENING, AND SERVING WINE

A good Margaux, a vintage Dom—there's no shortage of wine on the Upper East Side, even if we rarely get a peek inside anyone's cellar. And while this is a cocktail book focused on spirits, I'd be remiss not to briefly address the world of wine. After all, it's not a real party without something for everyone.

STORING WINE

It's a myth that *all* wine gets better with age, but most great wine does. Whether you're interested in starting a collection or just want one special bottle that you can break out at a casual 100-person house party or to celebrate being made the youngest editor in chief in media history, it's important to know how to properly store wine.

Wine is a dynamic, living thing, so treat it carefully. It is best to store wine in a cool, dark, and ideally, damp, place. If you don't happen to have an underground cellar or cool, dark closet, you can keep it in a moderately warm place. The best temperature for storing wine is 45 to 64°F, but 50 to 55°F is the ideal range.

Even more important than the temperature, though, is temperature consistency. A slightly warmer but consistent environment is better than a dark, cool place where the temperature fluctuates. Fluctuations can cause corks to expand and contract, leading to seepage and the possibility for too much oxygenation.

Corked bottles should be stored on their sides (to keep the cork wet). Screw cap bottles can be stored upright.

OPENING WINE

I recommend a simple, double-hinged wine key–style corkscrew over fancier, more high-tech options. Not only does it take up less storage space, but it also allows for more control.

To open a still wine, cut the foil wherever you want, though tradition dictates just under the lip. Rotate the corkscrew through the center of the cork. Using the shorter lever, pull the cork out halfway, then place the longer lever against the lip of the bottle and pull the cork the rest of the way out.

To open a sparkling wine, remove the foil capsule and untwist the wire cage. Keep the cage on the cork and hold both securely in your hand (use a tea towel for stubborn corks for more friction). Hold the base of the bottle with your other hand and slowly twist the bottle off the cork, rather than pulling the cork out of the bottle. NEVER push a cork out with your thumbs.

SERVING WINE TO GUESTS

Sharing a good wine can elevate a gathering from an ordinary dinner to a truly pleasurable experience. Think about the order in which you want to serve your wines, and make sure they are all at the appropriate temperature.

The temperature of wine when served matters just as much as the temperature at which it is stored. You can use the ranges below as a guideline for serving various types of wine.

❖ Champagne: 41 to 45°F

❖ White wines: 49 to 55°F (The lighter the white, the colder it should be to preserve acidity and freshness.)

❖ Rosé: 48 to 53°F

❖ Red wines: 62 to 68°F, or just below room temp

For wines that have been stored on their sides, make sure to right the bottle one to days before opening to allow the sediment to filter to the bottom. Here are some rules of thumb to consider in deciding the order of serving your wines:

- Serve younger wines first, followed by older vintages.

- White wines are typically served before moving on to reds.

- Lighter-bodied wines are a good usher before fuller-bodied wines.

- Serve sweet wines after dry wines, or you risk overpowering the dry wines.

Cheers, kittens.

CHAPTER 2

Gin
Cocktails

Martini Fit for a Queen

{AKA: GIN MARTINI}

Did you really think I'd start this book any other way? A classic martini. Gin, as it should be. The ultimate slumber party drink, or for being spotted in the Palace bar when you're about to make up with your long-lost best friend. But you better not even think about pouring this into a cocktail glass. A martini this elegant deserves a real martini glass.

2 ounces gin

½ ounce dry vermouth

green olives, for garnish

If you want it as dirty as the details one anonymous blogger serves up, splash a half ounce of olive juice in there as well.

In a chilled cocktail shaker, gently stir the gin and vermouth together with the ice cubes.

Strain into a chilled martini glass (glasses stored in the freezer are best) and garnish with olives.

Despite the Hollywood allure of ordering a martini "shaken, not stirred," a proper martini is always gently stirred. Shaking or vigorously stirring a martini breaks the ice and waters down your cocktail. Watery gin might be fine for a certain British spy, but a Manhattan Queen needs a more powerful punch.

A G6

This just in: a certain devil dismissed the angel on his shoulder and now that angel is forsaken for the summer. What better cocktail to drink on a private plane to Tuscany (or the jump seat of a private helicopter) than a classic Aviation? Gin is obviously the only spirit to lift yours when your not-quite boyfriend just stood you up without apology.

2 ounces gin

¼ ounce maraschino liqueur

¼ ounce crème de violette

½ ounce lemon juice (freshly squeezed)

1 flamed lemon peel, for garnish

Pour the gin, maraschino liqueur, crème de violette, and lemon juice into a shaker.

Add the ice and shake.

Strain into a cocktail glass.

Garnish with a flamed lemon peel.

> To really impress your guests, a flamed lemon peel is the way to go. Hold the lemon peel between your index finger and your thumb with the white pith facing out. Light a match and squeeze the peel into the flame. A quick burst of sparks as the citrus oils ignite will dazzle your guests and confirm that you flamed your peel correctly. But be careful—get too close to the flame and you might just get burned.

Hamptons White Party

{AKA: WHITE LADY COCKTAIL}

Ahh, summer in the Hamptons—sun, surf, and scandal. And, of course, no summer is complete until the annual White Party. If a Vitamin Water–sponsored cocktail isn't quite your cup of tea, go for a White Lady. Egg whites and lemon juice might not sound like the breeziest of summer soiree sippers, but you know the Hampton's elite doesn't mind a bit of sacrifice in service of a well-executed theme.

1½ ounces dry gin

¾ ounce triple sec

¾ ounce lemon juice

⅓ ounce Giffard sugar cane syrup

½ ounce egg white (¼ standard egg)

Fill a cocktail shaker with ice and add the gin, triple sec, lemon juice, syrup, and egg white. Shake well.

Strain into another cocktail shaker and shake without ice.

Pour into a cocktail glass.

The Bride's Your Mother

{AKA: BRIDE'S MOTHER}

Who doesn't love a high society wedding? The fanfare, the scandal, the booze? But when the bride's your mother and your future stepbrother is your ex-lover, you might need something a little bit stronger than Champagne, especially when the wedding day doesn't quite go as you planned. This spin on a Bride's Mother should do the trick.

1¼ ounces sloe gin

¾ ounce gin

½ ounce simple syrup

grapefruit slices, for garnish

 Pour the gins and simple syrup over the crushed ice in a cocktail shaker and shake vigorously.

Strain into a cocktail glass over crushed ice and garnish with the grapefruit slices.

XOXO A COCKTAIL BOOK

Dirty Scandal

{AKA: DUKE'S MARTINI}

When your boring rebound boyfriend turns out to be noble, you can celebrate His Lordship with a Duke's Martini. It's called a cocktail but it's mostly gin in a coupe glass. Go for a London Dry gin, of course.

3 ounces gin

2 drops vermouth

 Chill a cocktail glass and gin in the freezer.

Pour the chilled gin and dry vermouth over ice in a shaker. Shake well.

Strain into the chilled cocktail glass.

Delicious Temptation

Ah, the gimlet. Timeless, elegant, and sinfully delicious. This stunningly simple cocktail is the perfect complement to an evening of luxury. Or debauchery. You can take your pick, though I know of a certain club where you don't have to choose. See you there, behind the curtain.

1¼ ounces gin

1¼ ounces Rose's lime juice OR fresh ½ teaspoon lime juice for ½ teaspoon simple syrup

lime wedge

Classic

Stir the gin, lime juice, and ice together, then strain into a chilled cocktail glass.

Squeeze the lime over the top.

Contemporary

   2½ ounces gin

   ½ ounce Rose's lime juice

   lime wedge

Same process.

Blue Bloods

{AKA: BLUE-BLOODED}

¾ ounce gin

¾ ounce passion fruit nectar

4 cubes mango

1 to 2 teaspoons blue curaçao

Your pedigree might be nearly noble but this cocktail sure isn't. A true Upper East Sider wouldn't be caught dead with a bright blue tropical colada in hand, even if they are spending the weekend somewhere between Tulum and Turks and Caicos. But we can't all be born with silver spoons, can we? If you need a break from poise, class, and being an arbiter of taste, slip off your pearls and headband, throw a cocktail umbrella in this frozen concoction, and forget the pressures of being a Park Avenue princess for a short while.

 Blend the gin, passion fruit nectar, mango, and ice into a blender and blend until smooth.

Pour into a tall chilled glass and top with a floater of blue curaçao.

XOXO A COCKTAIL BOOK

Dorm Party Sake-tini

You know what they say: moving on ain't easy, especially when you're moving on below 14th street. You might still be Queen, but that doesn't mean your new subjects know it. What's a poor B to do? Throw an over-the-top bash, of course. These sake-tinis and a sushi bar might just be the key to downtown domination. Or they might just make you realize that your best days are behind you (when you wake up the next morning, that is).

1½ ounces sake

½ ounce gin

½ ounce triple sec

orange spiral

 Fill a cocktail shaker with ice.

Add all remaining ingredients to the shaker and stir.

Strain into a martini glass.

Bridge Burner

{AKA: BRONX COCKTAIL}

For all intents and purposes, the Bronx might as well not exist. Neither should Queens, for that matter. And, of course, we all wish we could forget about Brooklyn. But for the sake of fair play and because I just received a dirty dish, I'm feeling generous today, so here you go. A cocktail for the other borough of our fair city. Let's all raise a glass and a sigh of relief that S never made it across the bridges to the north. Or god forbid, to Staten Island.

1½ ounces gin

¼ ounce dry vermouth

¼ ounce sweet vermouth

¾ ounce fresh orange juice

orange slice, for garnish

 Shake the gin, vermouth, orange juice, and ice and strain into a chilled cocktail glass.

Garnish with the orange slice.

> The Bronx Cocktail was invented at the Waldorf Astoria when a customer dared barman Johnny Salon to invent a new drink on the spot. This was a popular option during Prohibition to mask the presence of alcohol. Salon named the cocktail after the Bronx Zoo, which he had visited earlier that day (god knows why).

High Society

{AKA: GIN AND TONIC}

Gin once had a bad rap for being an old lady's liquor, but not all old ladies are content to sip G&Ts at bridge club. If your grandma had spent years as a muse at Studio 54, schemes with the best of them, and is wily enough to realize she's being conned but goes along with it anyway, you might rethink your opinions about gin, too.

This simple cocktail really showcases the gin, so make sure you don't skimp. Tanqueray might be a key to happiness, but you could also try Hayman's. Feel free to drink straight from a tea cup if your family is grating on your nerves.

2 ounces gin

4 ounces chilled tonic water

1 to 2 lime wedges

Pour the gin and tonic water into a rocks glass filled with ice and stir.

Squeeze the lime wedges and then drop them into the drink.

Dressed to Kill

{AKA: TUXEDO}

1½ ounces gin

1½ ounces dry vermouth

¼ teaspoon maraschino liqueur

¼ teaspoon anise liqueur

2 dashes bitters

maraschino cherry, for garnish

Black tie, white tie...it's just another Tuesday for Upper East Sinners. Whether the occasion is an opening at the Metropolitan Opera, a decadent masquerade (or four), or just the final act of another epic takedown, you'll never go wrong with—or in—a Tuxedo. Clothes do make the man, just make sure to keep them on, and to keep a limit of two of these cocktails. You never know who's watching.

Fill a cocktail shaker with ice and add the gin, dry vermouth, maraschino liqueur, anise liqueur, and bitters. Stir well and strain into a chilled cocktail glass.

Garnish with a cherry.

XOXO A COCKTAIL BOOK

Members Only

Forget Hamilton House or *La Table Elitaire*, or even the Colonie Club. This is one club anyone can join. Which of course means most people worth having won't want to sign up. After all, what's the point of a club if it doesn't establish your supremacy over the rest of the huddled masses? Even if this particular club does not demonstrate your dominance, it will still go down smooth while you scheme and set your sights on a truly elite society.

1¼ ounces gin

¾ ounce lemon juice

¾ ounce grenadine

1 egg white

lime twist, for garnish

Fill a cocktail shaker with ice and add the gin, lemon juice, grenadine, and egg white. Shake vigorously until frosted.

Strain into a chilled cocktail glass and garnish with a lime twist.

Sir Thomas Collins

{AKA: TOM COLLINS}

1½ ounces gin

¾ ounce
lemon juice

¾ ounce
simple syrup

club soda

lemon wheel,
for garnish

Daniel, Carter, Nathaniel, Benjamin...now Thomas? A little birdie told me that our favorite serial monogamist has another new man in her life. Will this one stick around longer than the others? Only time will tell, but I'm guessing not, if even an Ivy professor or a long-lashed lacrosse player can't ride it out. On the other hand, maybe the answer isn't in a man at all, but rather at the bottom of a highball. Worth a shot—if a round through New York's finest hasn't yielded a man who can tame our wild lady, maybe poor Tom Collins is the comfort she's looking for.

Fill a shaker with ice and add the gin, lemon juice, and simple syrup. Shake vigorously and strain over more ice into a highball glass.

Top with club soda and garnish with the lemon wheel.

This drink is named after a popular hoax from the 1870s. Someone allegedly named Tom Collins would sit in a bar and loudly speak slanderously about another. The victim would hear that their reputation had been besmirched, show up at the bar, ask the bartender if they'd seen Tom Collins and would be handed a sour drink. I know we're all glad schemes have gotten more sophisticated.

Nemesis

They say that the quickest way to turn an enemy into a friend is to seek that enemy's council. And we all know there's no shortage of enemies on the Upper East Side. But if you don't have a suitable problem, or if you're just out of time on a scheme and need to flip a nemesis stat, you could always go for the second-quickest option: a premium cocktail and a shared intimacy. A Negroni is a crowd-pleasing cocktail, but complex enough to impress with your mixology skills.

1 ounce gin

1 ounce Campari

1 ounce sweet vermouth

2 to 3 ounces club soda (optional, others prefer to serve over ice)

orange slice, for garnish

Shake the gin, Campari, and vermouth with ice in a cocktail shaker, then strain into an ice-filled highball glass.

Top with club soda and garnish with the orange slice. Alternatively, you can strain the mixture into a cocktail glass and leave out the ice and club soda. For this version, garnish with an orange twist.

The Powerful Woman

{AKA: ROSEMARY GIN FIZZ}

FOR THE SIMPLE SYRUP:

½ cup water

½ cup sugar

2 rosemary sprigs

FOR THE GIN FIZZ:

2½ ounces gin

½ ounce lemon juice

3 ounces club soda

1 lemon slice,
for garnish

1 rosemary sprig,
for garnish

If you have a penchant for headbands, dream in scenes from Audrey Hepburn movies, and have recently evolved from a tyrannical teenager to the one person everyone is actually rooting for, I know you're going to love this next cocktail. There's nothing I respect more than a Powerful Woman, and when those words are used to describe what seems more like self-actualization and the reaching of potential, I'm in full support. Here's hoping our Queen and ex-princess one day makes it to the elegant, powerful woman she wants to be. I'll be watching, with this classic Gin Fizz in hand.

Combine the water and sugar in a small saucepan and heat over medium heat. Bring to a boil while stirring regularly.

Once the sugar is completely dissolved, remove the simple syrup from the heat and place one rosemary sprig in the simple syrup. Let the rosemary steep for an hour.

XOXO A COCKTAIL BOOK

After an hour, discard the rosemary sprig, pour the simple syrup into a jar, and refrigerate for an hour.

Add ice to a cocktail shaker. Combine the gin, lemon juice, and one tablespoon of the simple syrup in the cocktail shaker. Shake well and strain into a rocks glass over ice.

Top off with club soda. Garnish with a lemon slice and rosemary sprig.

Looking to add a unique tool to your bar? Try an infuser. A proper infuser will allow you to create any number of cocktails, syrups, or oils. Try infusing gin with rosemary sprigs over 2 to 3 days, and then use a basic simple syrup for this cocktail.

XOXO A COCKTAIL BOOK

One Kiss...

{AKA: SLOE KISS}

And that's that. I hear a certain duo is locking lips. Well, I suppose everyone is, aren't they? Whether it be for love, for hate, for revenge, or for sabotage, there are a million reasons for a simple little kiss. But the first kiss between former enemies-turned...well, what exactly they've become I don't quite know. Yet. But stay tuned. You know I'll be dishing the dirt as soon as it's shoveled.

1¾ ounces sloe gin

2 to 3 ounces orange juice

orange slice, for garnish

 Fill a cocktail shaker with ice, sloe gin, and orange juice. Shake vigorously until frosted, and strain into a rocks glass.

Garnish with the orange slice.

The Golden Shell

{AKA: SABRINA}

½ ounce gin

¾ teaspoon
apricot brandy

½ ounce fresh
orange juice

1 teaspoon
grenadine

1½ teaspoons
Cinzano

sweet sparkling wine

orange and lemon
slices, for garnish

Charlie, Derrick, Clair and, of course, we can't forget Sabrina. A word to the wise, Lonely Boy—if you're going to write a fictionalized tell-all about your chums, you might want to work a little harder to keep their real identities a secret, or risk being seen as the Brooklyn Benedict Arnold who bit the hand that's been feeding you. You'd think a novelist would get a little more creative in the naming department.

Pour the gin, apricot brandy, orange juice, grenadine, and Cinzano into an ice-filled cocktail shaker and mix. Pour into a champagne flute.

Top off with sparkling wine.

Garnish with orange and lemon slices.

XOXO A COCKTAIL BOOK

Monte Carlo Pact

{AKA: MONTE CARLO}

The great love isn't always the right love, but sometimes they are one and the same. All bets are off when years of on again, off again, and "it's complicated" finally start to wind down...until suddenly that moment comes and you go all in. An epic love story deserves an epic cocktail, and this one is even more delicious than finally finding your fairy-tale ending.

¾ ounce gin

¼ ounce white crème de menthe

½ ounce fresh lemon juice

3 to 5 ounces chilled Champagne

 Combine all of the ingredients but the Champagne in a cocktail shaker and shake vigorously.

Strain into a flute and top with champagne.

There are two ways to make this: an imperial (served in a flute, as above) and a highball (use 1¾ ounces gin and 1 ounce lemon juice).

CHAPTER 3

Whiskey, Scotch, & Bourbon Cocktails

Kiss on the Lips

{AKA: FRENCH KISS}

1¾ ounces bourbon

2 teaspoons grenadine

1 teaspoon lemon juice

You know GG is the ultimate insider on the Manhattan party scene, and for the underage crowd, there's no invite more coveted than one Kiss on the Lips. But no need to party crash, I hear the last KOL let just about anyone in—including not one but two poor babes from across the bridge. Could it be that the Queen's iron fist isn't as tight around the guest list as it used to be? Maybe one too many of these bourbon cocktails has loosened her up. Or is she losing her edge? Perhaps the time is coming for a hostile takeover.

 Pour the bourbon, grenadine, and lemon juice into an ice-filled cocktail shaker and shake vigorously.

Strain into a chilled cocktail glass.

XOXO A COCKTAIL BOOK

Up to No Good

With a name that draws on a famous Scottish outlaw, a Rob Roy is the perfect cocktail for an annual Lost Weekend—especially one where an outcast former insider makes his not-so-triumphant return. A cousin of the Manhattan and originally created in New York's Waldorf Astoria hotel, this oft-overlooked concoction is just the remedy for getting your pride run down at a backdoor poker game in Queens.

2½ ounces blended Scotch

1 ounce sweet vermouth

2 dashes Angostura bitters

 Fill a mixing glass with ice. Add ingredients and stir.

Strain and pour in a rocks glass with 1 large ice cube.

Robert MacGregor acquired the name "Roy" as a child for his mop of red curly hair. Made famous and glamorized by Sir Walter Scott, MacGregor was actually leader of the MacGregor clan. During the late-17th century and early-18th century, MacGregor and his men's racket-scheme offered cattle farmers "protection" in exchange for a fee.

Little J(ameson) and Ginger

{AKA: JAMESON AND GINGER ALE}

3 ounces Jameson

1½ cups ginger ale

Ireland might not be at the top of the list of most glamorous places to be photographed, but it did give us one thing to be thankful for: Irish whiskey. This cocktail might seem basic to you, but watch out for this one, darlings. You never know what danger might await you when you tangle with the J.

 Pour the Jameson into an ice-filled highball glass and top with ginger ale.

XOXO A COCKTAIL BOOK

Schemer's Delight

A French cocktail gets the Royale treatment in this spritzed version of a Sidecar. Cointreau and Cognac, both French liqueurs, pair naturally with Champagne, though any sparkler will do. Might I suggest grabbing a bottle from those three cases your ex-party pal had delivered to your school? Even a reformed bad girl needs a libation sometimes.

You can serve this in a Champagne flute, but it's also quite tasty in a cocktail glass rimmed with sugar.

1¼ ounces bourbon

¾ ounce Cointreau

1½ teaspoons freshly squeezed lemon juice

chilled Champagne

Fill three quarters of a shaker with crushed ice. Pour the bourbon, Cointreau, and lemon juice into the shaker and shake well.

Pour into a chilled flute and top with Champagne.

A Chilly Goodbye

{AKA: HOT TODDY}

½ cup bourbon

juice of ½ lemon

2 tablespoons honey

1 cup hot water

lemon wedge,
for garnish

cinnamon stick,
for garnish

When the weather turns cold, you know that's when things on the Upper East Side are just heating up. There's nothing like Thanksgiving to bring out the drama, as we've learned time and again. Thanksgiving weather in NYC might not be that frigid, but that doesn't mean the relationships aren't. When a cold shoulder freezes you out or you've been served an ice-cold dose of humiliation, this Hot Toddy is the perfect antidote to thaw you out.

 Add the bourbon, lemon juice, and honey to a clear glass mug. Top with hot water and stir.

Garnish with the lemon wedge and cinnamon stick.

For a spicy twist on this classic drink, use hot honey to add a kick!

Rosewood

{AKA: BOULEVARDIER}

1¼ ounces bourbon

1 ounce Campari

1 ounce sweet vermouth

orange twist, for garnish

As we age, our tastes often change. Where we used to like grunge rock and blue jeans, we now lean more toward gala events and YSL. Where we used to down cocktails and shots backstage, we now prefer to unwind on a spotless white couch with a glass of Burgundy. But sometimes our past comes screaming back to us, and there may come a time when you just need a strong cocktail. This Boulevardier is just the ticket. Basically a Negroni but with bourbon instead of gin, it's smooth, strong, and still classy as hell. The perfect cocktail, perhaps, to share with your Scotch-rocks type stepson when he drops by for a visit. Plus, your mother was always more of a gin drinker; so this, like you, is like a version 2.0.

The Boulevardier will be served over ice unless requested otherwise, but I recommend you order this shaken and served up for a cocktail you can savor.

 Stir all liquid ingredients in a mixing glass with ice, then strain into a rocks glass with ice or serve "up" in a cocktail glass and garnish with the orange twist.

When you order this by name and the bartender looks at you confused, tell him or her that you want a Negroni with bourbon.

Lady Alexander

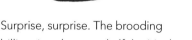

10 mint leaves

1½ teaspoons superfine sugar

large splash of seltzer water

2½ ounces Kentucky bourbon

crushed ice

mint leaf, for garnish

Surprise, surprise. The brooding billionaire who owns half the Manhattan skyline was more than a little shady. Color us shocked. But what exactly were his dirty deeds? A man doesn't fake his own death (and leave behind his mountains of cash) for no reason. The devil's in the details and our favorite dynamite duo is on the case.

Uncovering the biggest scandals often requires a field trip or two. Luckily, most dirty business is done somewhere you can get a decent cocktail. When you happen to visit the track on the trail of the truth, enjoy a delicious Mint Julep. It might not be the Vanderbilt charity polo match, but hey, any equine event deserves a little bourbon.

Place the mint leaves in a rocks glass and pour the sugar on top. Muddle together until the leaves begin to break down.

Add the seltzer water and bourbon. Fill the glass with crushed ice and give it a light stir.

Garnish with a mint leaf.

Victrola

1 teaspoon
absinthe or Pernod

2 ounces Cognac
(or bourbon or rye)

3 to 4 dashes
Peychaud's bitters

lemon twist

If you're going to open a successful club before you're even legally allowed to drink, it's going to require perfection. The perfect theme, the perfect vibe, every detail in alignment, straight down to the signature drink. And what's the signature cocktail of a speakeasy burlesque club to be? I'm thinking a Sazerac.

This cousin to an old-fashioned is made with rye and a wash of absinthe, the official liquor of sin. Combined with the fact that this cocktail originally comes from the Big Easy, it seems it's a natural fit for a wickedly hedonistic watering hole.

 Coat the inside of a chilled old-fashioned glass with the absinthe or Pernod and pour out any excess. Shake the Cognac and bitters with ice, then strain into the prepared glass.

Twist the lemon peel over the glass and drop it in if you want (purists wouldn't).

Invented in New Orleans in 1838, Antoine Amedie used a coquetier (also known as a jigger) to mix the first variation of this drink. Thus, the word "cocktail" was born!

A Bow on the Right

{AKA: WALDORF COCKTAIL}

1½ ounces bourbon

¾ ounce Pernod

½ ounce sweet vermouth

dash of Angostura bitters

They say friends are fashion fundamentals but "they" clearly don't know what they're talking about. Who needs friends when you have devoted minions, and the fearful respect of an entire city? It isn't easy being the reigning teen Queen of the Manhattan social dynasty; so after a long day of vendettas, meddling, and taking what you want, kick up your heels and relax with a delicious Waldorf Cocktail.

 Stir everything together in a glass, then strain into a chilled cocktail glass.

Some recipes swap the Pernod for ¼ ounce absinthe. Simply begin making your cocktail by pouring the absinthe into the glass. Swirl the absinthe around the inside of the glass to coat it and discard what is left.

XOXO A COCKTAIL BOOK

New York, I Love You

{AKA: NEW YORK SOUR}

New York, New York. We can't all make it here, nor should we. The most fabulous city in the world is basically another character in our favorite drama and has the personality to fit right in—a tough, glittering exterior, with just the smallest amount of warmth underneath to keep us hanging around. This cocktail celebrates the complexity that is New York, from the Upper East Side right down to 23rd Street (that's the only part of New York that matters, *n'est pas?*).

2 ounces bourbon

1 ounce freshly squeezed lemon juice

½ ounce sugar cane syrup

1 dash aromatic bitters

¾ ounce red wine, such as Bordeaux

Pour all ingredients, except wine, into a cocktail shaker filled with ice and shake vigorously until frosted. Strain into an ice-filled rocks glass.

Drizzle the red wine over the surface of the drink.

New York Spectator

1 sugar cube

2 dashes bitters

½ teaspoon grenadine

3 ounces bourbon

orange rind, for garnish

maraschino cherry, for garnish

This just in: every show needs a straight-edged sidekick and we find ours in one brooding, banged lacrosse player. A lower-key ladies' man with the weight of his world on his shoulders, our (comparatively) honorable vanilla snack often deserves a drink. But what would everyone's slightly off moral compass choose for his signature sipper? I'm placing my bets on an old-fashioned. Reliable and undramatic, but great for nursing in a dark bar while pining after one thing or another, this is one concoction you simply must master for a well-rounded portfolio.

Place the sugar cube in the bottom of a cocktail shaker. Add the bitters and grenadine.

Muddle until the sugar is mostly dissolved. Fill the cocktail shaker with large, unbroken ice cubes.

Pour bourbon over the ice. Stir well. Strain into a highball glass over a single large ice cube.

Light a match and lightly toast the orange rind over the flame.

Garnish with the orange rind and cherry.

Above 14th Street

There's nothing like a well-made Manhattan in fall. Or winter. Or spring, summer...this classic cocktail is as versatile and multifaceted as the island (and its inhabitants) for which it is named. And those inhabitants sure do get up to some mischief, don't they? But you know what they say: when it comes to a scandal, I'll take a Manhattan any day.

2 ounces whiskey

1 ounce vermouth

2 dashes bitters

orange rind, for garnish

maraschino cherries, for garnish

Fill a cocktail shaker with ice. Add the whiskey, vermouth, and bitters, and stir.

Strain into a highball glass over one large ice cube.

Rub the orange rind over the rim of the glass.

Garnish with the orange rind and cherries.

Life in the Fast Lane

{AKA: MOONSHINE MARTINI}

2½ ounces
moonshine

½ ounce vermouth

lemon twist,
for garnish

If you're launching a club named after a famous gin-based cocktail, it might make sense to serve gimlets as the signature drink the night of the opening. But then, you'll never make a bass-sized splash in the pond by doing the expected. And what could be more unexpected than a Moonshine Martini? An old bootlegger's spirit gets a refined twist with this simple two-ingredient concoction. Not too refined, though—let's not forget the club is on the Upper *West* Side.

 Fill a cocktail shaker with ice. Add the moonshine and vermouth, and stir.

Strain into a chilled martini glass. Add the lemon twist to garnish.

Devil's Delight

While a Scotch and Soda hardly counts as a cocktail, you know I can't get away with not including it here. There are too many glasses of Scotch downed in the six greatest years by our favorite well-bred degenerates to miss this opportunity. Normally I wouldn't waste a good Scotch by mixing it with club soda,

2 ounces Scotch

6 ounces club soda

but if you have an endless booze budget it hardly matters, and if it is before 2 p.m., the soda dulls the flagrant disregard for decorum by drinking hard liquor so early. Not that a minor transgression like that would ever *really* tarnish a reputation on the Upper East Side, of course. It takes more than a little partying to bring a titan down.

 Pour the Scotch into a highball glass filled with ice. Add club soda.

For a smooth and affordable Scotch and Soda, I recommend The Famous Grouse. If budget is no issue, splurge for an 18-year-old Glenlivet.

The Runner Up

{AKA: WHISKEY SOUR}

Spotted: a former lover fleeing to Vermont in disgrace. For years the best friend wanted to be the leading lady but was always playing second fiddle to one leggy blonde or another. And when she finally got her shot, she threw it all away in jealousy. There's nothing worse than when a friendship turns sour, but poor V never stood a chance. Turns out she's just a detour on true love's twisted quest.

2 ounces bourbon

1 ounce freshly squeezed lemon juice

¾ ounce simple syrup

1 egg white from a medium egg

maraschino cherry, for garnish

Add the bourbon, lemon juice, simple syrup, and egg white to empty cocktail shaker. Dry shake the ingredients.

Fill the cocktail shaker with ice and shake again.

Double strain over ice into a rocks glass by pouring it through the shaker's built-in strainer and into a mesh strainer. Garnish with a cherry.

A Brooklyn Backstabber

{AKA: BROOKLYN COCKTAIL}

1½ ounces rye

¾ ounce sweet
vermouth

dash of maraschino
liqueur

lemon twist,
for garnish

Brooklyn, Brooklyn. Whether you call it home or an unfortunate but necessary pit stop in service of a larger scheme, Brooklyn is a behemoth. Our friends on the Upper East Side might not realize there's more to the borough than one street in DUMBO and being the birthplace of the biggest snake in NYC, but I know you know better. This cocktail is a variation of a classic Manhattan but with rye instead of whiskey and lemon instead of orange.

 Stir all ingredients but the garnish together in a mixing glass, then strain into a chilled cocktail glass.

Run the lemon peel around the rim, then twist over the drink and garnish.

> In honor of this cocktail's namesake, I recommend Empire Rye whiskey. It is distilled at Kings County Distillery in the Brooklyn Navy Yard, just a stone's throw from a certain loft apartment on Water Street.

A Vicious Circle

Uh oh, Lonely Boy—you've finally been accepted by New York's literary elite, only to be rejected by the elite that really matters. Don't worry yourself so; I'm sure your friends will see the light through your dark side and come to celebrate with you. But, in the meantime, you have your agent, your new screenplay, and an ex– best friend and thief to thank for it.

    What better way to celebrate your literary acclaim than with a drink at New York's most famed literary haunt? But if you can't make it to the Algonquin Hotel in person, you can try this Algonquin cocktail instead. I can't say it will be quite as satisfying as drinking within the same walls as The Vicious Circle once did, but it's worth a shot.

2 ounces rye or blended whiskey

½ ounce dry vermouth

1 ounce pineapple juice

 Stir all of the ingredients in a mixing glass, then strain into a cocktail glass.

CHAPTER 4

Rum & Tequila Cocktails

Lonely Boy Beergarita

{AKA: BEERGARITA}

lemon wedge

salt

2 ounces tequila

1 ounce agave
nectar

1 ounce freshly
squeezed lime juice

6 ounces
Mexican beer

lime wedge,
for garnish

A sixteen-year-old who's uncomfortable with the high-society underage drinking thing? Definitely going for a beer. But this is a cocktail book, after all. Go for this twist on a margarita to comfort yourself the next time the love of your life makes it clear she doesn't know you exist, while plotting your way into ruining her life and capturing her heart. Bonus points for using a Brooklyn Lager, obviously.

Cut a slit horizontally across the lemon wedge, then rub the slit lemon around the rim of a chilled glass.

Sprinkle salt over a plate, then rim the glass by rubbing the juiced rim into the salt.

Pour the tequila, agave nectar, and lime juice into a shaker. Fill the shaker with ice and shake well.

Add the beer to the shaker and then strain into a glass over ice. Garnish with a lime.

  XOXO A COCKTAIL BOOK

Minion's Mai Tai

{AKA: MAI TAI}

1½ ounces
spiced rum

½ ounce
coconut rum

1 teaspoon
grenadine syrup

3 ounces
pineapple juice

2 ounces
orange juice

After a long day of being barked, bossed, and bitched at by a royal B, sometimes you just need to unwind with one or three delicious rum painkillers. I can't help but wonder how a tyrant collects so many minions—is it just the access and allure? Or is she holding something over your head? Maybe a fourth Mai Tai and you'll let the secret slip.

Fill a cocktail shaker with ice. Add the spiced rum, coconut rum, grenadine, pineapple juice, and orange juice and shake well.

Strain over ice into a highball glass.

Inner Circle

{AKA: MOJITO}

Mojitos at Socialista for your 15th birthday on a school night? That's how you know you've made it with Manhattan's elite. That is, until you put a toe out of line and realize revenge, like the perfect mojito, is frequently served ice cold.

2 sprigs mint, plus more to garnish

¾ ounce lime juice

¾ ounce simple syrup

crushed ice

2 ounces white rum

club soda

Clap the mint together in your hands to release the aromas. Add the mint to the bottom of your drinking glass.

Pour the lime juice and simple syrup over the mint and muddle the ingredients.

Fill three quarters of the glass with crushed ice. Pour the rum over the ice and stir well.

Top off with club soda and garnish with mint leaves.

The Embezzler

{AKA: STRAWBERRY DAIQUIRI}

Oh Captain, the Captain. Someone did a bad, bad thing and is trying to avoid his just deserts. Fleeing to the Caribbean to avoid a social faux pas is one thing, but fleeing the law is another entirely. Didn't anyone tell you that "fugitive" isn't a good look? But if you insist on living it up while lying low, you might as well enjoy a delightful frozen daiquiri. Maybe three will be enough to help you forget how you threw your family to the sharks.

2 ounces light rum

1 ounce lime juice

½ ounce triple sec

½ teaspoon granulated sugar

½ cup thinly sliced strawberries, plus more to garnish

1 cup ice (optional)

 Add the rum, lime juice, triple sec, sugar, and sliced strawberries to a blender. (Add ice for a frozen daiquiri.) Blend well.

Pour into a chilled margarita glass and garnish with strawberry slices.

Down to Her La Perla

1¼ ounces tequila

½ ounce raspberry liqueur

½ ounce crème de cacao

¾ ounce heavy cream

cracked ice

fresh raspberries, for garnish

Tequila might not be your favorite spirit, but no cocktail is more fitting than a Silk Stockings for when your broken heart compels you to perform at your friend's new burlesque club. You know what they say—you can't keep a bad girl down, but this playful mixture goes down smooth as, well, silk.

An alternate suggestion: substitute cinnamon for garnish, grenadine instead of raspberry liqueur, light cream instead of heavy cream.

Pour the tequila, liqueurs, and cream into a shaker. Fill the shaker with cracked ice and shake well.

Strain into a chilled cocktail glass and garnish with raspberries on a toothpick.

The Coveteur

You might think the upper crust of Manhattan society would be content with their bountiful blessings, but even the people who have everything sometimes wish for what they *don't* have. I know you know that envy is just one of the deadly sins committed on a daily basis around here, but it can certainly be the most toxic. You can't always get what you want, but that doesn't mean it is okay for anyone else to have it. But careful what you wish for, darlings. Covet thy neighbor and you might get more than you bargained for.

1½ ounces tequila

½ ounce blue curaçao

¼ ounce pineapple juice

maraschino cherry, for garnish

 Fill a cocktail shaker with ice. Add the tequila, blue curaçao, and pineapple juice.

Shake well and strain into a chilled cocktail glass. Garnish with a cherry.

Talk of the Town

{AKA: HURRICANE}

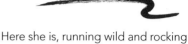

2 ounces silver rum

2 ounces gold rum

2 ounces passion fruit juice

1 ounce orange juice

simple syrup

grenadine

lime juice

orange slice, lime slice, and maraschino cherry, for garnish

Here she is, running wild and rocking your world. It's often said that in the eye of a hurricane there is quiet, but for just a moment until her glamorous, dramatic life sweeps you away again. She loves sequins, short skirts, and pretending to be good now, but we all know that there's no doubt about the signature cocktail for this ex-Queen, former bad girl. No matter what she tells you or where she runs, the drama is never far behind. And I hear she wouldn't have it any other way.

A little silver, a little gold, and an equal amount of passion (fruit) is the recipe for this cocktail that originated in the Big Easy. Toss in some sugar and fruit and you have a gorgeous, and deadly delicious, drink on your hands.

Pour the rum and juices into an ice-filled shaker. Add a splash of simple syrup, grenadine, and lime juice. Shake well until frosted.

Pour into a tall cocktail glass and garnish with the orange slice, lime slice, and cherry.

XOXO A COCKTAIL BOOK

Red-Hot Revenge

{AKA: HOT BUTTERED RUM}

Spotted: one former insider getting the cold shoulder and a frosty reception. I guess your friends aren't as forgiving as you thought they'd be. Poor baby. You could pack up your bags and admit defeat. Or you could kill them with kindness. But there's always our favorite tactic for melting a cold heart: blackmail. There's nothing like a little tit for tat to warm friends up and bring them around. After all, nothing bonds on the Upper East Side like being under each other's thumbs.

1 teaspoon soft butter

1 teaspoon brown sugar

dash of allspice

dash of ground cinnamon

dash of ground nutmeg

splash of vanilla extract

2 ounces dark rum

5 ounces hot water

Combine the butter, brown sugar, allspice, cinnamon, nutmeg, and vanilla extract in the bottom of a clear glass coffee mug and muddle well.

Add the rum, and then hot water.

Stir and serve.

On-Again, Off-Again

{AKA: DARK AND STORMY}

2 ounces Gosling's
or Myer's Dark Rum

5 ounces
ginger beer

lime wedge,
for garnish

When a blackout rolls across Manhattan and you get stuck in an elevator with your newly-on-again (for now) boyfriend, nothing captures the spirit of the time like a Dark and Stormy. You might think you've finally kicked that judgy do-gooder to the curb, but watch out: history tends to repeat itself, right down to the very same elevator.

Pour the rum and ginger beer into an ice-filled highball glass.

Squeeze a quarter of a lime into the glass. Stir.

Garnish with a lime wedge.

Baby Mama

{AKA: BAHAMA MAMA}

1 ounce light rum

1 ounce gold rum

1 ounce dark rum
(if it is after 2 p.m.)

2 ounces
pineapple juice

2 ounces
orange juice

splash of grenadine

pineapple wedge,
for garnish

maraschino cherry,
for garnish

So your college freshman girlfriend suddenly scores a high-profile internship at CNN for three months in Haiti—and abandons you. Don't worry darling, you won't be lonely for long. I hear your Brooklyn loft has a revolving door, and now our favorite chaos-raining firecracker is back, and boy does she have a bombshell for you. Could it be that after your fling last fall when she walked away or ran away, she took a piece of you with her there?

What'll it be, D? Will you grow up overnight, or will you let the sparks fly off again?

 Fill a cocktail shaker with ice. Add the light rum, gold rum, dark rum, pineapple juice, and orange juice.

Shake well and strain over ice into a tall glass. Splash grenadine over the top.

Garnish with a pineapple wedge and cherry.

Queen B and Her Bitches

Ah, sabotage and scheming, two of Manhattan's most historic pastimes. But it isn't just the ladies who get a little shady. Men, children, even Brooklynites—no one is safe from the thrall of executing the perfect scheme. You might think you can resist, but when something threatens what you want, you know you'll turn in a minute. Don't worry, darling, I'm certainly not one to judge. In fact, let's celebrate embracing your shadowy side with this tequila brew. I'll drink to that.

2½ ounces tequila

¾ ounce apple brandy

¾ ounce cranberry juice

splash of lime juice

 Pour the tequila, apple brandy, cranberry juice, and lime juice into an ice-filled cocktail shaker. Shake vigorously.

Strain into a chilled cocktail glass.

Take It Easy

2½ ounces
aged tequila

1 cup orange juice

1 teaspoon
grenadine (or
raspberry liqueur)

maraschino cherry,
for garnish

It's another tequila sunrise to comfort you when you realize you're a "nostalgic" B-level rock star just trying to be a good dad and usually not pulling it off. No one will tell you, but you need to just chill out, stop being so rigid and judgmental. And maybe just relax with a drink. Or perhaps a joint with your bassist. Put on an Eagles vinyl, chat with the wife you don't deserve, and just let everyone live.

 Pour the tequila over a tall cocktail glass filled with ice. Add the orange juice and gently stir.

Add grenadine over the center of the glass so that it slowly descends down the glass.

Garnish with a cherry.

> While Patron never fails, sometimes you need a less expensive tequila. For a more affordable bottle, consider the award-winning Espolòn Blanco tequila.

The Palm Beach Impostor

{AKA: PALM BEACH}

¾ ounce white rum

¼ ounce gin

¾ ounce
pineapple juice

pineapple slice,
for garnish

It isn't every day you bump into your long-lost cousin and invite her to come live with you, only to later realize she's actually an actress from Florida who was hired by your aunt to steal family money, after which she went to live with your grandmother on her deathbed, only to resurface once more at the hospital alongside your real cousin, then crash your grandma's wake, inherit her entire fortune, before discovering your cousin's father is actually *your* father. I've been in the secrets business a long time now, but sometimes even I am surprised and confused by the drama you Upper East Siders have going on. It's amazing that you're able to get anything done.

But I appreciate industry as much as the next girl, so here's a Palm Beach recipe to toast to that poor little Floridian who somehow managed to claw her way up even higher than the van der Woodsens. *Salud.*

Fill a cocktail shaker with ice and add the white rum, gin, and pineapple juice. Shake vigorously until frosted and strain into a cocktail glass.

Garnish with a pineapple slice.

XOXO A COCKTAIL BOOK

Rumor Has It

There's nothing better than a takedown, except maybe a white-hot fling. On the Upper East Side, more business is done in the bedroom than the boardroom and *les liaisons dangereuses* are just another Tuesday afternoon. We all know that the hottest stars burn out the fastest and that's certainly true for the trysts of high society. What burned bright one day leaves you cold the next. But this cocktail will stay true.

A Between the Sheets will of course require a flamed citrus, so be careful and don't get too close to the fire, or risk getting burned.

1 ounce cognac

1 ounce triple sec

1 ounce light rum

¼ ounce lemon juice

flamed orange peel

Fill a cocktail shaker with ice. Add cognac, triple sec, rum, and lemon juice.

Shake well until frosted and strain into a chilled cocktail glass.

As you serve, flame an orange peel over the glass and drop it in the drink.

Lola's Libation

{AKA: DAIQUIRI}

2 ounces light rum

1 ounce freshly squeezed lime juice

1 ounce simple syrup

lime slice, for garnish

Her name was Lola, and she was a show-biz girl...that is, until she was suddenly an Upper East Sider. Nothing says newly refined It-Girl with Florida roots like a daiquiri. A little bit classy, a little bit let your hair down, a true daiquiri is fitting for any number of occasions. Discovering a long-lost family? I prescribe two. Inheriting a trust fund? A celebratory six. Finding out your dad is your uncle and your mom hired your friend to impersonate you? Oh my, skip the lime and just hit the rum from the bottle.

Fill a cocktail shaker with ice. Add the rum, lime juice, and simple syrup, and shake well.

Strain into a chilled cocktail glass and garnish with a lime slice.

XOXO A COCKTAIL BOOK

Pre-Marriage Margarita

{AKA: MARGARITA}

A joke for you, loyal readers: What's the difference between Kir Royales at the St. Regis and margaritas at Panchito's for your bachelorette party? Two hundred plebeians and an arrest record. Poor bride, I hope those margaritas were worth an hour in jail. I can say for sure this one is.

lime wedge

coarse salt

4 ounces tequila

2 ounces Cointreau

2 ounces fresh-squeezed lime juice

½ ounce agave syrup

 Rub the edge of a chilled margarita glass with a juiced lime rind.

Rim the glass with coarse salt.

Fill a cocktail shaker halfway with ice. Add the tequila, Cointreau, lime juice, and agave syrup.

Shake vigorously and strain into the margarita glass.

Garnish with a lime wedge.

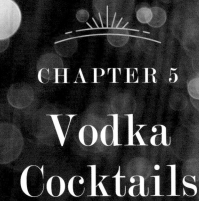

CHAPTER 5

Vodka
Cocktails

Billionaire Brunch

{AKA: BLOODY MARY}

2 ounces vodka

4 ounces tomato juice

1 dash Worcestershire sauce

1 dash hot sauce (such as Tabasco)

½ teaspoon horseradish

⅛ teaspoon fresh cracked pepper

1½ teaspoons lime juice

1 tablespoon lemon juice

1 celery stalk (with the leaves), for garnish

Wakey wakey, Upper East Siders, it's Sunday morning in Manhattan. And you know what that means: anyone who's anyone is going to brunch. But for the city's elite, brunch isn't casual and you better not show up with last night's eyeliner still on. For billionaires, brunch is just another opportunity to seal the next deal. You can't be seen with any old cocktail in your hand, and we all know that mimosas are sooo Brooklyn. Try a classic Bloody Mary instead, with Belvedere vodka, naturally.

 Add all of the ingredients except the celery stalk to a shaker filled with ice. Stir and strain into a glass.

Add celery stalk to garnish.

There is much debate over who actually invented this classic hangover cocktail. However, popular theory credits Fernand "Pete" Petiot. It is believed he invented the Bloody Mary while working at Harry's New York Bar in Paris. Yet another cocktail that marries New York and Paris—how serendipitous.

 XOXO A COCKTAIL BOOK

A Summer at the Cape

{AKA: CAPE CODDER}

One bad season might not be quite enough to make you never want to summer in Newport again, but after two, you might be considering the Cape. This cocktail is the perfect accompaniment to closing up your family's yacht for the season.

2 ounces vodka

4 to 5 ounces cranberry juice

½ ounce fresh lime juice

lime wedge

Shake the vodka, cranberry juice, and lime juice together with ice in a chilled metal cocktail shaker.

Strain into a highball glass filled with ice.

Squeeze the lime over the drink and then garnish.

Up in Flames

{AKA: KAMIKAZE}

1½ ounces vodka

1 ounce lime juice

1 ounce triple sec

lime wedge,
for garnish

Named after a specific group of World War 2 Japanese pilots, the Kamikaze doesn't mess around. Bold and bracing, but not particularly complicated or enjoyable, this shot sets out to destroy. It'll get ya drunk and make sure you don't remember it. Much like one bombshell we all know who pops up from time to time to create mass chaos before slinking back into the shadows. For the easiest encounter, this should be served like her heart and her blood—ice cold.

Fill a cocktail shaker with ice and add vodka, lime juice, and triple sec.

Shake well and strain into a chilled cocktail glass.

Garnish with a lime wedge.

Call Me Serena

Rumor has it long-lost family is coming back with a vengeance, and it's not all fun and games. They say imitation is the sincerest form of flattery, but the original S better watch her back, or she might get replaced in everyone's affections.

 Pour all of the ingredients except for the cherry into a shaker filled with ice. Shake vigorously.

Strain into a tall cocktail glass filled with crushed ice.

Garnish with a cherry.

1¼ ounces Ketel One vodka

1¼ ounces coffee liqueur

1¼ ounces Disaronno Originale Amaretto

1¼ ounces Baileys Irish Cream liqueur

1¼ ounces single cream

1¼ ounces 2% milk

maraschino cherry, for garnish

A Dirty Dish

{AKA: DIRTY MARTINI}

Martinis, secrets, and aired laundry—just about the only things I think are better when they're dirty. There's no shortage of ways to make a martini but I know you won't be surprised to learn that I prefer them extra dry and doubly dirty. Personally, I take the recipe below and swap the measurements for olive juice and vermouth, but if you can't handle it, I understand. Not everyone can hang with the big girls.

2 ounces vodka

½ ounce extra-dry vermouth

¼ ounce olive juice

green olive, for garnish

 Mix the vodka, vermouth, and olive juice in an ice-filled cocktail shaker.

Stir and strain into a martini glass.

Garnish with an olive.

Scorched Earth

{AKA: 151 ABSOLUT FLAME}

1½ ounces
Absolut vodka

splash of lime juice

splash of grenadine

splash of
Bacardi 151

Sometimes you're a Park Avenue Princess and the world is your oyster. And other times you're a little Brooklyn wannabe clawing her way up, making one bad decision after another. And then still other times, you're a shell of your former Brooklyn self, well on your way to burning your life to the ground thanks to a healthy heaping of self-sabotage. Whether you need a torch for a trash can fire full of bespoke dresses, or just a shot of lighter fluid to send your old life up in flames, 151 has the ABV you need. But torch carefully, darling, not all fires can be put out.

 Add vodka, lime juice, and grenadine to a small glass and stir. Pour into a shot glass.

Pour Bacardi 151 over the back of a small spoon so that it layers on top of the shot.

Light a match and set the shot on fire. (Quickly extinguish, see page 116.)

XOXO A COCKTAIL BOOK

Attempt this drink at your own risk, and know that flaming drinks can be dangerous (even more dangerous than a tango with a hothead model). Should you decide to ignite your spirit, take note of a few things:

❖ The only truly safe way to extinguish a flaming shot is by smothering it with an upside-down coffee mug. If you blow it out you risk blowing flaming alcohol out of the glass.

❖ If you leave the shot on fire long enough, the shot glass could shatter/explode.

❖ The shot and shot glass may be very hot after the flame is extinguished.

❖ Any alcohol more than 80 proof will ignite. The higher the proof, the easier it is to set it on fire.

XOXO A COCKTAIL BOOK

Elegant Woman

When you turn 18 on the Upper East Side, you must cast aside your childish playthings. For a certain little bee, that means embodying the poise, elegance, and Grace of another American princess. Forget the Beluga and Belvedere, there's nothing classier than a martini, and this one has an unexpected twist (in case you're getting tired of regular martinis and expected twists). The blood orange pairs well with $18 peonies and not needing presents because you already have literally everything.

4 cups blood orange juice

2 cups orange-flavored vodka

1 cup orange liqueur

1 cup simple syrup

black sanding sugar

blood orange slices, for garnish

 Combine the blood orange juice, orange-flavored vodka, orange liqueur, and simple syrup in a large pitcher. Refrigerate until chilled.

Serve in martini glasses rimmed with the black sanding sugar.

Garnish with the blood orange slices.

Lady in Waiting

{AKA: WHITE RUSSIAN}

Rise and shine, kitten, your lady's maid is here with breakfast in bed and an ever-forgiving attitude. No queen can shine without her faithful servants, her loyal confidante, and her humble valet, and for the reigning royalty on the UES, all those jobs fall to one long-suffering matron.

1 ounce vodka

1 ounce coffee liquor

1 ounce heavy cream

After years of raising, taming, and reining in a little tyrant, our poor housemother has earned a hard-won drink. Everyone knows she has a penchant for vodka, and while Poland isn't Russia, I believe Russian by marriage counts. And the shot of coffee liqueur in a White Russian might give our beleaguered right-hand woman the energy she needs for disguises, accents, and snooping.

Fill a rocks glass with ice. Pour the vodka and coffee liquor over the ice and stir.

Pour the heavy cream over the top of the drink.

Double Trouble

{AKA: COSMOPOLITAN}

1¾ ounces vodka

¾ ounce triple sec

¾ ounce lime juice

¼ ounce
cranberry juice

Substitution:
Swap triple sec
for Cointreau
orange liqueur.

It might not be the most high-brow of concoctions, but a Cosmo is a standby you need to have in your bar-senal. When your ex– party mate "Svetlana" suddenly comes out of the woodwork looking for her partner in crime, nothing will get her dishing like this. Nothing but Belvedere here, obviously, unless you want the "sparks" to fly.

Fill a cocktail shaker with cracked ice.

Pour the remaining ingredients over the ice and shake vigorously until well frosted.

Strain into a chilled cocktail glass.

Belvedere never fails, though it can be costly to keep Belvedere on your bar. While I know that's not a real issue, you may consider Tito's for a more economic vodka staple.

Svetlana's Downfall

It only takes two to tangle in the making of this cocktail, similar to some other activities I can think of. You should be wary of tangling with anyone on a flight to Minsk though—you never know who you might upset, or what extra baggage you might disembark with.

2 ounces Kahlua coffee liqueur

1 ounce vodka

 Pour liqueur and vodka into a mixing glass filled with ice.

Stir the ingredients and then pour over fresh ice into a rocks glass.

Minsk Mule

{AKA: MOSCOW MULE}

2 ounces vodka

1 ounce fresh
lime juice

12 ounces
ginger beer

fresh mint,
for garnish

lime wedges,
for garnish

Paris is the place to be for love and heartbreak, but there's no doubt that Russia holds the gold for the place to execute a vicious vendetta. If you're being banished (or potentially offed) by your recently dead father, a tearful goodbye and Casablanca-level romantic kiss on the tarmac in front of a plush company plane will have to hold you over 'til you can plan the perfect revenge. Betrayal is a bitter pill to swallow, but this Moscow Mule helps it go down easier.

Pour the vodka and lime juice into 2 copper mugs, filled with ice.

Fill both mugs with ginger beer.

Stir and garnish with fresh mint and lime wedges.

XOXO A COCKTAIL BOOK

The Ultimate Source

{AKA: VODKA MARTINI}

Who am I? I always said that's one secret I'd never tell, but sooner or later, all good things must come to an end, and that includes my reign of terror. We had a good run, didn't we, darlings? We laughed, you cried, and it certainly made life more interesting.

2 ounces vodka

½ ounce dry vermouth

lemon twist or green olive, for garnish

But some secrets are real doozies and if you're caught off guard, allow me to recommend a strong drink to steady your nerves. You could go for a tequila shot or a stiff Scotch, but I'd take my page from the book of one devoted lady's maid: vodka on the rocks, a big glass, with not too many rocks and three olives.

But if that isn't quite your style, try this vodka martini instead. The vermouth helps soothe the burn of the vodka. Though I know you love a good burn. And you know you still love me.

 Stir the liquid ingredients in a mixing glass with ice, then strain into a chilled cocktail glass.

Garnish with the lemon twist by running the peel around the rim and then twisting over and dropping into the drink, or with the olive.

For a dirty martini, add a dash of olive juice.

CHAPTER 6

Wine Cocktails

Butter Than Revenge

3 ounces white
peach puree

4 to 6 ounces
chilled prosecco

peach slice,
for garnish

Nothing keeps a Queen down for long,
even if an upstart Brooklynite thinks she's
got her beat. When your pack stands you
up, grab a Bellini, put on a brave face,
and start plotting. Sooner or later they all
bow down or bow out, and you've been
craving a good challenge.

Pour the peach puree into a chilled Champagne flute
and top with prosecco and a peach slice.

First created in Venice, a traditional Bellini is made with pureed
fresh white peaches, which can be hard to find. In a pinch, you can
use peach nectar, but you know the Upper East Side won't settle
for anything less than the best.

Ivy Week Refreshment Committee Punch

{AKA: ROSÉ BERRY BLISS PUNCH}

1 750-milliliter
bottle of rosé

½ cup blueberries

½ cup blackberries

12 ounces frozen
pink lemonade

1 liter lemon
lime soda

Spotted: one lonely boy manning the refreshment table, rather than schmoozing for his big chance to go Ivy. If you can't dazzle with your witty conversation, you might as well slay with a punch. None are pulled in this boozy recipe.

 Pour the rosé, blueberries, blackberries, and pink lemonade into a punch bowl and stir. Refrigerate covered for at least 1 hour.

Pour into champagne flutes, filling two-thirds of the glass.

Top off with lemon lime soda.

Golden Girl

Golden hair, a sunny smile, and fat bricks of bullion in your mom's safe upstairs. When you've been blessed with a silver spoon and a gilded life, the world is your oyster. Pick the pearls you want and cast the rest before the swine.

¾ ounce gold rum
½ ounce Cointreau
chilled Champagne

This dazzling cocktail mixes Champagne, Cointreau, and gold rum—a luxurious and delightful combination. Cheers to the girl in the gold cotillion dress, the one everyone wants to be or talk about, the legend who shines brighter than all the lights of Manhattan. Here's looking at you.

 Pour the rum and Cointreau into a champagne flute and top off with Champagne.

Make sure you are using *actual* Champagne. Champagne comes from the Champagne region of France and is often made with chardonnay, pinot noir, or pinot meunier grapes.

Summer in the Hamptons Sangria

{AKA: TRADITIONAL WHITE SANGRIA}

1 lime

1 lemon

½ green apple

1 peach

6 strawberries

¼ cup cane sugar

¼ cup apple brandy

1 (750-milliliter) bottle Albariño wine

3 cups frozen berries

No one does summer like New Yorkers, and you'd better grab your sunblock, sweetie, because this one's a scorcher. You might think the Hamptons is nothing but big houses, couture, and fabulous parties and, well, you're right. When the days get longer, Manhattan's elite flee east for sun, surf, and…a bit of something else. But you know a scandal's not a scandal without a cocktail to enjoy it with, so mix up a batch of this sangria, pull out your Prada sunnies, and sit poolside while you monitor your favorite gossip blogs.

Cut the lime, lemon, apple, peach, and strawberries into thin slices. Add the lemon and lime to a large pitcher.

Add the sugar and muddle with a wooden spoon. Add the apple brandy and muddle again. Add the apple, peach, and strawberries and stir well. Add the wine and stir well.

Add frozen berries to chill just before serving.

  XOXO A COCKTAIL BOOK

The Huddled Mimosas

{AKA: MIMOSA}

2 ounces fresh
orange juice

¼ ounce Cointreau

3 to 5 ounces
sparkling wine

Rise and shine, kittens, it's time for Sunday brunch in Brooklyn, where the booze may be bottomless, but it certainly isn't top-shelf. Anyone can sling an OJ and prosecco flute, but this mimosa recipe goes the extra mile. Use bottled orange juice if you must, I know most of you across the bridge don't have a lady's maid waiting in the wings with a pitcher of freshly squeezed.

 Pour the orange juice and Cointreau into a chilled flute and top slowly with sparkling wine.

XOXO A COCKTAIL BOOK

Art Gallery Opening Punch

{AKA: WHISKEY FRUIT PUNCH}

If you just can't handle one more glass of warm Yellow Tail Shiraz at your dad's art gallery's latest opening party, try this punch instead. The juice and brandy will help mask the flavor of whatever commercial wine he brought in. Because, let's face it, that certainly isn't a Dom '98.

1 (750-milliliter) bottle cherry whiskey

12 ounces strawberry liqueur

6 ounces passion fruit juice

1 (750-milliliter) bottle Champagne

strawberries, for garnish

lemon twists, for garnish

Pour the cherry whiskey, strawberry liqueur, and passion fruit juice into a punch bowl. Cover and refrigerate for an hour.

Add chilled Champagne just before serving.

Ladle into champagne flutes and garnish with the strawberries and lemon twists.

If you come across a liqueur called Passoã, grab it. This French-made passion fruit liqueur is a fun way to dress up this punch.

Park Avenue Princess

{AKA: GIN FIZZ ROYALE}

2 ounces gin

1 ounce fresh
lemon juice

1 teaspoon sugar

2 to 3 ounces
Champagne

A royal cocktail made with gin and Champagne—do I really need to explain? I hope I don't also have to tell you that the only acceptable brand of Champagne is Dom Pérignon. Anything less and I wouldn't expect a seat at the table.

Shake the gin, lemon juice, and sugar in a mixing glass with ice, then strain into an ice-filled highball glass.

Top with Champagne and stir gently.

An I Love Paris Sigh

{AKA: FRENCH 75}

Oh la la. Paris, nous t'aimons. What a joy it is to be in France, whether you're about to take over your mother's atelier, or just trying to live a peaceful, humble life after a brush with death. One can't help but utter a little sigh of relief to be home again.

1¾ ounces gin

¾ ounce lemon juice

chilled Champagne

Just as with the country, there's nothing quite like a French 75. The noblest of spirits is lightened up with *la crème de la crème of bubbles. C'est tres magnifique.* Any soiree improves when you have one of these (or two) in hand.

 Fill a cocktail shaker with ice and add gin and lemon juice. Shake vigorously until frosted.

Strain into a white wine glass and top off with champagne.

If you are looking for the true historical origin of this particular cocktail, enjoy the hunt, because there is no shortage of legends. What we do know is that the French 75 first appeared in print in 1927 in a New York humor magazine. The French 75 is the only classic cocktail who's origin dates back to Prohibition.

The Harry Winston

{AKA: DIAMOND FIZZ}

2 ounces dry gin

1 ounce lemon juice

½ ounce sugar cane syrup

Brut Champagne

Diamonds are a girl's best friend, especially when that diamond is a Gibraltar-sized symbol of betrothal. Whether it is from a lost Dark Prince or a sunny Monégasque one, I hear that Upper East-size sparkler could be seen from space.

This particular diamond might not be from Fifth Avenue, but nothing could be more fitting to celebrate the future marital bliss of the Queen of the Upper East Side (and possibly a small European municipality).

Fill a cocktail shaker with ice and add gin, lemon juice, and sugar cane syrup.

Shake well and strain into a chilled champagne flute.

Top with champagne.

Femme Fatale

They say we only run from the things that truly scare us: showing up to a white tie event in black tie, discount stores, and developing budding feelings for your nemesis were heretofore the only things that could be classified as such, but here's a new one to add. This cocktail, the Kir Lethale. If it doesn't scare you yet, honey just wait. Tomorrow morning you'll be wishing you'd run away faster than a Hollywood starlet when the paparazzi showed up.

1 raisin

1 teaspoon vodka

½ ounce crème de cassis

sparkling wine

Soak the raisin in vodka for at least an hour. Place raisin at the bottom of a cocktail champagne flute.

Pour the crème de cassis and any remaining vodka into the flute.

Fill the glass with sparkling wine.

Ultimate Insider

{AKA: APEROL SPRITZ}

3 ounces prosecco

2 ounces Aperol

1 ounce soda water

orange slice,
for garnish

There's nothing like a summer in Tuscany, writing a book with a nemesis, when you're supposed to be at a prestigious fellowship in Rome. I hear the hottest new novel in town was written by an unlikely duo. I guess it's true what they say—alcohol heals all wounds, even those inflicted by scheming moms to not-your babies.

Ah well, the days over the typewriter may be long and the company less than appealing, but it's no match for the Tuscan sun and free-flowing prosecco. If you can't make it to Italy to live the life of a renaissance writer, perhaps you can re-create the feeling with everyone's favorite summer sipper.

 Pour the prosecco, Aperol, and soda water into a white wine glass over ice.

Stir and garnish with an orange slice.

XOXO A COCKTAIL BOOK

Intimate Soiree

An elegant and intimate bachelorette party? I know just the thing. There's nothing that screams tasteful celebration like a Kir Royale. And the fact that you're celebrating your impending royal-dom is a touch that doesn't go unnoticed. Just make sure to keep an eye on your glass—even I don't know what lengths a spiteful princess will go to in service of her vendetta.

6 ounces Champagne or prosecco

½ ounce crème de cassis

lemon twist, for garnish

 Pour the Champagne into a Champagne glass.

Add the crème de cassis.

Garnish with a lemon twist.

> If you are not interested in splurging on Champagne, use prosecco. Prosecco is a Northern Italian sparkling white wine made from the Glera grape. It will offer a more affordable yet dry and sophisticated alternative to the classic Champagne.

Heartbreak on the Left Bank

{AKA: DEATH IN THE AFTERNOON}

1½ ounces absinthe

4 ounces Brut Champagne

We all know Paris is never a bad idea, but a summer in Paris with your best friend to get over a broken heart? Now that's the sort of Parisian affair we'd want to remember. Brunch at Rôtisserie du Beaujolais on Ile de Saint Louis and shopping in the Seventh are all well and good in the morning, but if the afternoon doldrums set in and you catch yourself feeling lonely, this cocktail is the perfect antidote. A favorite of the perpetually melancholy Hemingway, this might be just what you need to finally take the bull by the horns, find that new man to make you feel sparkly, and get over your ex once and for all.

 Pour the absinthe into a champagne flute.

Fill the glass with Champagne.

A word of advice? Be careful with this one—absinthe, unlike some people—doesn't play games. Don't say I didn't warn you.

Bisoux Bisoux

{AKA: ST-GERMAIN AND CHAMPAGNE}

Boys and fortunes may come and go, but a best friend is forever. Usually. Unless you're waging yet another war against each other. But for times when there's peace in the kingdom and all you want is manicures, macarons, and a good dish session, a St-Germain and Champagne is the perfect complement. It may not be your favorite cocktail from Les Très Particuliers, but I bet this sophisticated drink will have you reminiscing about your halcyon days on the Left and Right Banks (respectively) of Paris in no time.

2 ounces
St-Germain liqueur

Brut Champagne

strawberry slice,
for garnish

Pour the St-Germain liqueur and champagne into a champagne flute and stir.

Garnish with the strawberry slice.

CHAPTER 7

Other Spirits & Liqueur Cocktails

The Metropolitan Steps

{AKA: METROPOLITAN}

1½ ounces brandy

1½ ounces sweet vermouth

½ teaspoon simple syrup

2 dashes Angostura bitters

maraschino cherry, for garnish

You probably shouldn't be seen sipping a Metropolitan on the steps of the Met, particularly if you're underage, or risk igniting a scandal. But on the Upper East Side, a life without scandal is no life at all, so go ahead and flout decorum and open-container laws, if that's what pleases you today.

 Gently stir all liquid ingredients in a cold glass with the ice, then strain into a chilled cocktail glass and garnish with a cherry.

There are two ways to make a Metropolitan, this classic way and the other *nouveau* variation. I think we all know which way is correct (after all, there's only one Met) but I'll include the other way as well (see page 177) in case you need to court a Five Families group of overprivileged, under-trustworthy teen queens.

XOXO A COCKTAIL BOOK

Hampton Jitney Iced Tea

{AKA: LONG ISLAND ICED TEA}

We're obviously not talking about a Hamptons cocktail here, and the only acceptable drink on the North Fork is wine. But there is a whole other world to pass through on the Jitney, and they need alcohol there, too. Though, if you're on the Jitney, rather than in a private helicopter or at the very least a town car...well, you probably need a drink, too.

1 ounce vodka

1 ounce gin

1 ounce white rum

1 ounce tequila

½ ounce triple sec

2 tablespoons freshly squeezed lemon juice

½ cup cola (or to taste)

2 lemon wedges, for garnish

Fill a shaker with ice.

Pour the liquid ingredients in the shaker. Shake well.

Pour into 2 highball glasses and garnish with the lemon wedges.

Frosty Weather

{AKA: BOOZY SKINNY HOT CHOCOLATE}

Cue the trumpets, strumpets, it's
Christmastime in the city. And you know
what that means: more than just five
golden rings. No one does anything like
Upper East Side does anything and that
includes Christmas. It's not winter on the
Upper East Side without two things: the
Snowflake Ball and window shopping
Fifth Avenue with a Jacques Torres hot
chocolate in your Gucci-gloved hand.
But forget the displays at Macy's, we're
more about that Bendel's life. This recipe
may not be *la crème de Jacques*, but
it does have a little extra holiday spirit
to help you forget the troubles of high
society.

2 cups unsweetened
almond milk
(or 2% milk)

5 teaspoons
cocoa powder

⅛ teaspoon
maple syrup

1 ounce Amaretto

Add the milk and cocoa powder to a saucepan over
medium heat.

When warm, but before boiling, add the maple syrup.
Stir with a whisk until boiling.

Once boiling, let simmer for 5 minutes.

Pour the Amaretto into two mugs (or one large mug).
Pour hot chocolate into the mug.

Teenage Casanova

{AKA: CASANOVA}

pinch of cayenne pepper

¼ teaspoon ground ginger

½ ounce bitters

2 ounces brandy

½ cup freshly squeezed orange juice

Ah, the Casanova—a little sweet, a little sour, and definitely the smallest bit spicy. Sound like anyone we know? While an OJ cocktail isn't as classically romantic as a bottle of Dom, this one is just complex enough to impress any date of an underage Lothario. Pairs well with a piercing squint and a near-constant whisper.

Add the pepper and ginger to a rocks glass. Add the bitters and brandy.

Chill in the freezer for 30 minutes.

Stir in the orange juice.

Jealous Lover

Nothing brings out the green-eyed monster in high school like seeing your ex with a new lover. Well, nothing except maybe the newest Hermès bag you're still on the waitlist for. In the face of jealousy, some resort to scheming, some go for sabotage, and still others resort to writing pining, sentimental short stories that somehow get published in the *New Yorker*. But us? I say nothing cures a bout of jealousy like a little hooch.

1 teaspoon crème de menthe

¾ ounce heavy cream

1¾ ounces coffee liqueur

chocolate matchstick, to serve

 In a measuring cup or wide glass, whip the crème de menthe and heavy cream with a fork or small wire whisk until thick.

Pour the coffee liqueur into a chilled shot glass, and then carefully add the whipped mixture over the liqueur.

Serve with a chocolate matchstick.

A Scheme and a Scandal

{AKA: SIDECAR}

lemon wedge

superfine sugar

1½ ounces Cognac or brandy

¾ ounces Cointreau or triple sec

¾ ounces fresh lemon juice

lemon twist

You know me...there's nothing I love more than a scheme and a scandal, and nothing that earns my respect like a girl who has her way with an antic.

Everyone needs a team-up for executing the perfect plot, whether it's the whole gang or just one loyal sidekick. The Sidecar is the ultimate cocktail to celebrate the Queen of Scheme and her plus one in subterfuge, whomever that might be this week.

 Rub the rim of a cocktail glass with the lemon wedge and rim with the sugar.

Combine all remaining liquids in a shaker with ice and shake to mix.

Strain into the glass and twist the lemon peel on top.

This classic cocktail comes with many variations. If you are new to the drinking scene, consider trying a Gosling's Sidecar. Made with a base of dark rum, this sweeter version makes for a great introductory cocktail.

Dangerous Liaison

2 ounces absinthe

1 sugar cube

10 ounces ice water

Oft-vilified, maligned, and misunderstood, absinthe might as well be the signature beverage for many people we know. It's a little daunting, I know, but take a walk on the dark side with this dangerously delicious absinthe cocktail. The key to absinthe is this: too much is just the right amount. But you better watch your back and remember there's always somebody watching.

 Pour the absinthe into a cocktail glass.

Place an absinthe spoon across the top of the glass, and place the sugar cube on the spoon.

Place the ice water in the absinthe fountain and place the absinthe and sugar cube under the absinthe fountain.

Slowly drip the water onto the sugar cube until the sugar is completely dissolved into the absinthe.

Anyone who knows absinthe knows that it is not meant to be shot and is not meant to be drunk straight. Unless you're mixing it into a cocktail, you should dilute it as described above, or risk a mixture that is *trop dangereuse*.

A Brazilian Fling

If Paris is for lovers, where do you go for a spicy spontaneous getaway with a new flame? Why, Rio of course. I hear our favorite blonde birdie flew the coop for a winter down south…and she wasn't alone. No doubt she's in for a few weeks of samba, sun, and sin. Not to mention more than a little cachaça. This Bossa Nova cocktail is the perfect mixture to make you feel sunny, even if you are left behind in the icy heart of a New York winter.

1½ ounces cachaça

1 ounce Frangelico

½ ounce Cointreau

¾ ounce fresh lime juice

¾ ounce cranberry juice

1 tablespoon honey

½ cup of ice

2 cranberries, to garnish

lime wedge, for garnish

 Combine ingredients except the cranberries and lime wedge in a blender, then blend until smooth.

Pour into a cocktail glass and garnish with the cranberries and lime wedge.

Saturday Night Shandy

{AKA: LEMON SHANDY}

Saturday nights, a movie and noodles in your dad's Brooklyn loft with your best friend slash girlfriend. Could one newly not-lonely boy perhaps be stuck in a rut? Your posh peers are all out trying new things and you have an evening routine at the age of 19. Sounds like you need to shake things up. But just in case you're not quite ready to stray too far from your comfort couch, this next cocktail is easy, delicious, and uncomplicated. And I only mean that a little bit as a snub.

10 lemons

2 cups sugar

1½ cups cold water

light lager beer (Peroni, or similar)

 Zest the lemons without removing the white pith. Juice the lemons and add it to a saucepan.

Add the sugar and water to the saucepan and apply medium heat, stirring regularly until the sugar is completely dissolved.

Remove from the heat just before the mixture begins to boil.

Pour into a mason jar and chill in the refrigerator for at least 1 hour.

Pour beer into a chilled pint glass. Add concentrate to the beer one tablespoon at a time to taste. (Three tablespoons recommended.)

Doctor's Dirty Shot

{AKA: CEMENT MIXER}

1 ounce Bailey's
Irish Cream

1 ounce lemon
or lime juice

They say blood is thicker than water—even if it shouldn't be. Not all daddies deserve their daughter's undying devotion, and we all know one doctor who should've stayed estranged.

The cement mixer shot is a classic bartender's trick, often served to patrons who need a nudge out the door. I don't recommend actually drinking this shot, but it might be a good recipe to have on hand for guests who, like pesky dads who refuse to give up and leave their families to the peace they've finally found, may have outstayed their welcome.

 Pour the Irish cream in a shot glass and layer with the lime juice.

Take the shot and hold in your mouth for 10 seconds before you swallow (if you can).

XOXO A COCKTAIL BOOK

Vivier Slipper

{AKA: FRENCH MONACO}

Could the Upper East Side tradition of scheming really be contagious? First it took down no one's favorite Brooklyn family, and now it looks like it has its hooks in our new-in-town Prince Charming. Is fairy-tale love enough to keep away the ghosts of schemes past, or will this dream come true end in a nightmare? I'll be watching...with a French Monaco in hand.

4 ounces amber beer

2 ounces lemon-lime club soda

¼ teaspoon grenadine

 Chill a tall beer glass.

Add beer, soda, and grenadine and stir.

Summer Romance

{AKA: CAIPIRINHA}

4 to 5 lime wedges

2 teaspoons sugar

2 ounces cachaça

If you're sunning in Capri or sinning in Croatia, or perhaps having a fling in Brazil, a Caipirinha is the answer—and not just to the question of what's one of the 10 most acceptable restaurants to be seen at on a Tuesday in Manhattan. Recalling the taste of a South American summer is the perfect remedy for any kind of blues—winter, heartbreak, or otherwise.

 Muddle the lime wedges and sugar in an old-fashioned glass until the sugar is dissolved in the juice.

Fill with ice and add the cachaça, then stir briefly.

The national cocktail of Brazil, the Caipirinha translates to "little country girl." The original iteration of this drink is believed to be cachaça, honey, lemon, garlic, and honey, and was used to combat the Spanish flu.

XOXO A COCKTAIL BOOK

The Princess Bride's Stepfather

{AKA: RUSTY NAIL}

1½ ounces whiskey

¾ ounce Drambuie

A stepfather walking his stepdaughter down the aisle on her fairy-tale day—it's almost enough to melt even the jaded heart of yours truly. Almost.

It would be inconceivable not to include a special drink for the best father figure on the Upper East Side. He might be short, a hugger, and have a catchphrase, but that's "not enough" to keep him from eventually softening his stepdaughter's heart. Though his first child may have turned out to be more thorn than rose, it looks like the second time's the charm. Even if this stepdaughter does occasionally require a nudge back to the straight and narrow.

The Rusty Nail cocktail didn't really become popular until the Rat Pack picked it up in crooner days. But I think this old-school, highbrow classic would appeal to most dads.

Combine the whiskey and Drambuie in an old-fashioned glass, fill with ice, and stir.

Of Course I Love You

{AKA: P.S. I LOVE YOU}

Five words. Sixteen letters. And a fairy-tale romance goes up in flames, just as another epic romance gets further from its happy ending. If the love between The Dark Prince and his elegant Queen is wrong, then I don't want to be right and you know GG agrees, no matter how many hurdles she's thrown their way.

While this little phrase doesn't mark the beginning of a happy ending, I hold out hope. So I'll be watching, sipping a cocktail toast, and trying to remember that sometimes, the hard way is the only way.

¾ ounce Irish cream liqueur

¾ ounce Amaretto

¾ ounce Bacardi Carta Oro rum

½ ounce coffee liqueur

 Add all ingredients into an ice-filled cocktail shaker. Shake vigorously.

Strain into another shaker and shake again without ice.

Strain into a chilled cocktail glass.

Uptown, Downtown

{AKA: PIMM'S CUP}

1½ cups Pimm's No. 1

1 navel orange, sliced into thin, circular slices

1 lemon, sliced into thin, circular slices

¾ cup packed mint leaves

1½ cups ginger ale

1 cucumber, cut into eight wedges

1 apple, quartered, cored, and cut into thin slices

What happens when the Ultimate Insider teams up with the Ultimate Catch? Apparently, nothing good. Poor babies, don't you know that Uptown and Downtown just don't mix? But if you insist on trying to carve out a place for your misbegotten romance, a highbrow salon is as good an idea as any...until it all goes awry.

God might save the Queen, but even He can't save your relationship. But your party just might be salvaged with a well-mixed cocktail. Try a Pimm's Cup for a British bash. Classier than a room temperature lager but easy enough not to scare off any of the lower-tier guests.

 In a large pitcher, combine the Pimm's No. 1, orange and lemon slices, and mint leaves. Chill for about 10 minutes and then add the ginger ale.

Place 2 cucumber wedges into 4 pint glasses and fill halfway with ice. Divide the Pimm's mixture and apples among the 4 glasses.

XOXO A COCKTAIL BOOK

Titan of Industry

{AKA: VANDERBILT}

Of course brandy is the main spirit in a cocktail named for a titan of industry. After all, nothing says "powerful" like a snifter of brandy in the smoking room. But you don't have to be a scion of an American dynasty to enjoy a Vanderbilt cocktail. Just shake everything together and prepare to feel outrageously affluent. For a real trip, use Cognac, a particular kind of brandy from a specific region of France.

1½ ounces brandy

1½ ounces cherry brandy

3 dashes Angostura bitters

1 teaspoon simple syrup

Shake together all the ingredients and strain into a chilled cocktail glass.

The Vanderbilts were titans of the railroad and shipping industry. When Cornelius Vanderbilt died in 1877, he was the richest man in America. The same can be said for his son William when he died in 1885. Their family once owned 10 prominent mansions along New York's Fifth Avenue. One present-day well-known Vanderbilt is none other than Anderson Cooper.

A Campbell Apartment

{AKA: SLOW COMFORTABLE SCREW AGAINST THE WALL}

1 ounce sloe gin

1 ounce vodka

1 ounce Southern
Comfort whiskey

2 ounces
orange juice

1 dash Galliano
liqueur

orange slice,
for garnish

maraschino cherry,
for garnish

Oh my, don't we ever learn from our mistakes? Cuckold a Queen once, dear, and live to tell the tale. But cuckold twice, and at the same venue no less, and your friendship might never recover. And once your escapade is broadcast via video at this year's debutante ball, your reputation might not either.

 Pour the gin, vodka, whiskey, and orange juice into an ice-filled cocktail shaker. Shake well.

Transfer to a tall, ice-filled cocktail glass. Dash with Galliano liqueur.

Garnish with an orange slice and a cherry.

Sloe gin is probably not the gin you first tried when pillaging your parents' liquor cabinet. This gin is a red liquor made with gin and sloe drupes, a small, red, plum-like fruit. Sloe gin is going to give your cocktail a much sweeter flavor while still providing the earthy qualities of a traditional gin.

God Save the Dons

{AKA: NOUVEAU METROPOLITAN}

Nothing is quite as nice as it was in your halcyon days, when you ruled the Met steps and no one was more relevant than your gang. They say you can't go back again, and it turns out they're right. When you discover that your legacy has been overshadowed by mob references and young upstarts with no loyalty, you might take to your bed and mope it out. Or you could beat these prima Don-nas at their own game.

2 ounces brandy

1 ounce sweet vermouth

½ teaspoon simple syrup

2 dashes Angostura bitters

Fill a cocktail shaker with ice and add the brandy, vermouth, simple syrup, and bitters.

Shake well and strain into a chilled cocktail glass.

CHAPTER 8

Mocktails

The Kids Are Alright

{AKA: LAVENDER LEMONADE}

6 cups water

½ cup colored honey

5 tablespoons dried lavender, gently crushed

1 cup fresh lemon juice

lemon slice, for garnish

Manolos, Cartier, Stella...in the glitz and glamour surrounding the upper crust of Manhattan, it is easy to forget that, technically, you're underage. If you're new to this world of no limits, no rules, or if you just happen to be at a party with judgy parents, here's a batch bevvy that walks the line of being delicious, but not sinfully so.

 Add the water and honey to a saucepan. Bring to a rolling boil over medium heat.

Add the lavender to the honey water and pour into a glass jar. Refrigerate for at least 2 hours and then strain out the crushed lavender.

Add the lemon juice and stir.

Serve in a tall glass and garnish with a lemon slice.

If you don't care about the legal drinking age, or if you're a real Upper East Sider, you can booze this up with a splash of vodka. Should you happen to own an infuser, try infusing some vodka with lavender.

XOXO A COCKTAIL BOOK

Sixteen Going on Seventeen

{AKA: SPARKLING PEACH SUNRISE

4 ounces lemon lime soda

3 ounces fresh peach juice

¾ ounce grenadine

peach slice, for garnish

Drinks with your UES frenemies might be your preferred celebration for turning Sweet 16, but daddy has other plans in mind. There's nothing more ho-hum-phrey than Rice Krispies treats and a family celebration at the loft. Is this Sparkling Peach Sunrise delicious enough to save the night? Or does a party this embarrassing require a little something extra? I'll be watching to find out.

 Fill a glass with ice and add the lemon lime soda. Pour the peach juice over the lemon lime soda and do not stir.

Slowly drizzle the grenadine over the top of the drink.

Garnish with a peach slice.

XOXO A COCKTAIL BOOK

The Barely Legal

{AKA: STRAWBERRY CITRUS FIZZ}

1 cup sugar

1 cup water

½ cup quartered
fresh strawberries

6 ounces lemon
lime soda

lime slice or
strawberry,
for garnish

Sometimes you need to hang up your razor-sharp Louboutins and your increasingly dramatic eyeliner and remember you're still actually a kid. The sweetness of this Strawberry Citrus Fizz will be just the ticket to remind you of the joys of being a teen. Pour a cold glass and settle in for a family board game night.

Add the sugar and water to a saucepan, and slowly boil until the sugar is completely dissolved. Let the strawberries steep in the syrup for an hour. Remove the strawberries and set them aside.

Fill a highball glass with ice. Add the lemon lime soda and top off with the strawberry simple syrup.

Garnish with a lime slice or strawberry and the macerated strawberries.

XOXO A COCKTAIL BOOK

Headbands and High School

{AKA: LIME RICKEY}

8 ounces lime juice

4 ounces
simple syrup

12 ounces
seltzer water

lime slices,
for garnish

A wise and frustrated mother once said that the difference between being an adult and being in high school is being able to mask your feelings. In other words, calm the eff down and get through an event without blowing it up, even if you don't feel like it.

It can be tough to be a teen on the Upper East Side, but being an adult there doesn't seem to be any easier. So until you can grow up and tamp down your emotions, you're relegated to the kid's table. A tough pill to swallow, but this Lime Rickey is easy.

Mix the lime juice and simple syrup in a measuring cup.

Fill 4 highball glasses with ice. Divide the lime and simple syrup mixture between the 4 glasses.

Top off each glass with the seltzer water and garnish with a lime slice.

  XOXO A COCKTAIL BOOK

The Derrick

{AKA: GINGER LIME FIZZ}

Little brothers are often ignored, while their big sisters are unfairly adored. Poor little vee-dubs couldn't buy, barter, or steal a moment of his own, and eventually he took the hint and skipped off to London for two or three years. But I think "Derrick" got an unfair shake—first in an insider's novel that pared him down to half a character and then by everyone else each time they refused to let him be anything other than second fiddle to one blonde bombshell or the other.

I'm raising my glass to little bros everywhere—maybe once you turn 21, people will start to care about you. But in the meantime, here's a Ginger Lime Fizz to soothe your spirit.

12 ounces
ginger beer

4 ounces
seltzer water

1 ounce lime juice

lime slice, for
garnish

 Add the ginger beer, seltzer water, and lime juice to a pitcher and stir well.

Pour into a pint glass over ice and garnish with a lime slice.

Drinks Index

Photo Credits

glassware throughout © Svitlana
  Medvedieva

page 6 © eatyurvegtables

pages 7, 21, 51, 77, 105, 129, 153,
  179 © Bokeh Blur Background

pages 4 to 11 © vectorpocket

page 20 © RoxTravels

page 22, 125 © Anna_Pustynnikova

page 24 © armano777

page 26 © Gilberto Villasana

pages 30, 58, 61, 79, 81, 93, 101,
  118, 122, 138, 142, 163 © Brent
  Hofacker

page 34 © Kalashnyk Serhii

page 36 © food

page 41 © etorres

page 42 © Evgeny Karandaev

page 45 © Candice Bell

page 50 © Kutsenko Denis

page 57, 121 © Shyripa Alexandr

page 62 © Joshua Resnick

page 67 © sanneberg

page 68 © Micaela Fiorellini

page 72 © Becca Eley

page 76 © Angela Aladro mella

page 82 © Jukov studio

page 84 © Elena Veselova

page 89 © wavebreakmedia

page 90, 108 © Oksana Mizina

page 97 © Evgeny Karandaev

page 102 © pilipphoto

page 104 © NewFabrika

page 107 © jefftakespics2

page 112 © Wollertz

page 115 © Maddas

page 126 © Evgeny Karandaev

page 128 © Ekaterina Kondratova

page 131 © Rimma Bondarenko

page 135 © Wiktory

page 137 © Natalia Van Doninck

page 141 © Oksana Mizina

page 147 © Goskova Tatiana

page 148 © Ekaterina_Molchanova

page 152 © Anna Nass

page 155 © Andrew Pustiakin

page 156 © Andrei Mayatnik

page 158 © Sea Wave

page 166 © photosimysia

page 171 © Rafael Trafaniuc

page 178 © Daintyfood

page 181 © Anna Puzatykh

page 183 © Ekaterina Kondratova

page 185 © Mirage studio

Acknowledgments

Thanks first to Casie Vogel, the beautiful, brilliant editor who came up with this book idea, and to Claire Sielaff, Claire Chun, Renee Rutledge, and Jake Flaherty, who helped make it great. And to Tyanni Niles, Juana Castro, Ashten Evans, Keith Riegert, and Ray Riegert for being fantastic colleagues who don't judge me for the amount of time I spent talking about alcohol.

Biggest thanks of all to Andrew Vigliotta, who didn't bat an eye when I texted him "I might've signed on to write a book in the next few months," and who supported the project in all ways, from mixing cocktails while I wrote to rewatching the entire six seasons of *Gossip Girl*. And for being just the best and having facial parts that are in all the right spots.

And thank you to Reba and Jeff Thoreson who have always encouraged me to pursue my interests in book publishing, writing, and drinking. Or if not encouraged, at least didn't stop me.

Thanks and love to Ann Kaiser, my soulmate and #1 hypeman forever. And to Kathryn, Angela, Megan, Norm, and Ben—for you, I'll try to make my next book about murder.

More thanks and love to Andrew again. Because he's swell and I want everyone who reads acknowledgments in the back of a pop culture cocktail book to know it.

About the Author

Bridget Thoreson once played pool with Chace Crawford in a bar and pretended she didn't know his name, which is what makes her qualified to write this book. If Bridget were any character from *Gossip Girl*, she'd want to be Lily van der Woodsen from seasons 1 to 4 or Blair Waldorf from seasons 4 to 6. In reality, though, she would, in fact, probably be Nate Archibald but not as pretty. Bridget's favorite cocktails are Kir Royales and Brooklyns and while her friends sometimes refer to her as B, they never call her their Queen. She lives in Brooklyn (by choice).